Native American Traditions

Written by Sydnie Meltzer Kleinhenz

Celebration Press

Parsippany, New Jersey

Long ago Native Americans fished and hunted. They gathered vegetables and grains. They made the clothes and the tools that they needed to live.

The first Native Americans didn't shop in stores as people do today. Everything they needed came from nature.

Today Native Americans don't always rely entirely on nature, but they do remember how their families lived long ago. Many of them teach their children about the history and traditions of their people.

Although the Native Americans of long ago spoke many different languages, they shared many ideas. They believed nature was alive and had feelings. Many Native Americans today share these same beliefs.

They teach their children to respect nature in many ways. For example, some Native Americans in the Pacific Northwest, which now includes Washington; Oregon; and British Columbia, Canada; believed that salmon gave themselves as food to hungry fishermen.

Even today these Native Americans traditionally return a fish skeleton to the river each year. They do this to show their respect for nature and to honor the salmon that helped their ancestors survive the long, dark winters.

Other traditions center around dancing. Some Native Americans in the Southwest, where Arizona and New Mexico are now, believed that dancing while thinking good thoughts brought good to everyone.

Hopi kachina dancers still perform at ceremonies held each February in Arizona. The dancers traditionally leave kachina dolls to remind children how to behave.

Giving gifts is another tradition. For a wedding or other important event, Native Americans in the Pacific Northwest hold a potlatch. The hosts give the guests food and gifts at this party. Our word *potluck* comes from this traditional gathering. Potlatches are also called Giveaways.

Traditional potlatch gifts

A modern potlatch

Storytelling is a tradition as well. Many Native Americans teach their children by telling them stories and legends. The Iroquois Indians of the Northeast lived in what is now New York State, Pennsylvania, and Quebec and Ontario, Canada.

They told a story of a bragger who fell and banged his face. After that his face was crooked. The bragger stopped bragging and began helping sick people get well. Some Iroquois still give traditional masks of crooked faces to sick people to help them get well.

A youth performing at a powwow

Native Americans often share their traditions at get-togethers called powwows. They make new friends and hold dance contests.

Native American life today is much different than it was long ago. But many parents still teach their children about the old times so that the traditions live on.